Table of Contents

Introduction 1
God's Solution to Worry, Anxiety, and Fear:
Part One 2
Part Two 6
Part Three 9
Part Four 13
Part Five 17
Part Six 23
Part Seven 28
Part Eight 32
Part Nine 36
Part Ten 40
A prayer for us all 43
Prayers 45
    Remember Who is in Control 46
    Prayers of Thanksgiving 48
    Prayers for God's Peace 51
    Prayers for our Minds 55
    Prayers for Distraction 58
    Prayers for Discipline 60
    Prayers for Help 62
    Prayers for Situations 64
    Prayers About Uncertainty 66

Modern Psalms for Worship 68
Proclamations of Faith...74
More Bible Verses for Your Peace and Comfort 79

Dedicated to all who suffer from worry, anxiety, and panic

Copyright © 2020 by Nathan Haddock

All rights reserved. This book, or any portion thereof, may not be reproduced or used in any manner without the express written permission of the publisher and except for the use of brief quotations in a book review.

Introduction

When troubles come, when worry and anxiety overwhelm us, when panic and fear attack, it can all seem overwhelming. However, God has a solution, an antidote if you like. No matter how bleak or frightening things seem, God is still in control, He is still sovereign, not distant but here for us all. He wants you to know His peace, hope, and even His joy during these troublesome times. This short book will help as you discover God's solution to worry, anxiety, and fear. Full of biblical teaching and practical advice, my prayer is that God will use this to bring you to peace and, like He has done for many others, turn your life around for the better.

Part One

Philippians 4: 4-9

Rejoice in the Lord always.
I will say it again: Rejoice!

God is amazing, He is so much more than we can ever imagine. He has given us so much to be thankful for. We sometimes forget the multitude of things that we have to give thanks for. Here we are told to remember; to give thanks at all times; to lift our heads from what we have not got, to focus on what we have. We can always find things to grumble about and tend to forget the hundreds of things we can be thankful for, even amid our worst fears and anxieties.

The verse is a reminder to...

   Remember who God is and give Him His due.

Remember what He has done for you in the past.

Remember that He is faithful.

Remember that He is in control

Remember, He created all things and knows the end from the beginning.

Remember to lift your eyes from your problems to God, the solution.

Remember to be thankful - for in being thankful, we usher ourselves into the presence of God

When we draw near to God by entering His gates with thanksgiving and praise, there is no better place for us to be. When we draw near to God, fear is cast out. When we enter His presence, all our troubles are seen in a completely different light. When the God of all creation is at our side, then our problems are lessened. We have someone with us to help us cope, to give us wisdom, and to go through them with us.

Remember to…

Give thanks at all times, in all places, and in all circumstances.

Lift your eyes from your problems to God, your solution.

Bible Verses to Meditate on

Psalm 32:11

Be glad in the LORD and rejoice, you righteous ones; And shout for joy, all you who are upright in heart.

Psalm 67:4

Let the nations be glad and sing for joy; For You will judge the peoples with uprightness And guide the nations on the earth

Psalm 68:3

But let the righteous be glad; let them exult before God; Yes, let them rejoice with gladness.

1 Peter 1:8

...and though you have not seen Him, you love Him, and though you do not see Him now, but believe in Him, you greatly rejoice with joy inexpressible and full of glory

Romans 12:12

Be joyful in hope, patient in affliction, faithful in prayer.

Psalm 40:16

Let all who seek You rejoice and be glad in You; Let those who love Your salvation say continually, "The LORD be magnified!"

Part Two

Philippians 4: 4-9

Let your gentleness be evident to all.
The Lord is near.

Gentleness is a wonderful attribute to develop. We have all met those with this wonderful gift. Those whose words, touch, and actions are gentle. They exude peace and calm, attributes from which we could all benefit. They can be at peace in the middle of chaos, and when we are with them, they help us to be at peace too. We can develop gentleness when we look to Jesus. He is gentle and at peace, and when we are with Him, in His presence, we are too. As we rest in Him, His gentleness will spread. As we sit at His feet, listen to His voice, read His Word and meditate on it, gentleness will rise in us. That gentleness will then be evident to others.

There is a calmness that spreads like wildfire. Just like panic spreads, so does calm. When everything is going wrong for us or those we love, God longs to draw near to us and bring us calm. When we are gentle, calm, loving, kind, God is near; not only to us but near to those around us. That is a promise that is worth holding onto in times of worry, stress, and anxiety. If we react in gentleness, then God draws near, and we all need that when these storms of life hit.

Remember to…

Be kind and gentle towards one another.

Hold on to the promise that God will draw near.

Bible Verses to Meditate on

Colossians 3:12

Therefore, as God's chosen people, holy and dearly loved, clothe yourselves with compassion, kindness, humility, gentleness, and patience.

Proverbs 15:1

A gentle answer turns away wrath, but a harsh word stirs up anger.

Galatians 5:22-23

But the fruit of the Spirit is love, joy, peace, forbearance, kindness, goodness, faithfulness, gentleness, and self-control. Against such things, there is no law.

Psalm 34:17-18

The righteous cry out, and the Lord hears them; he delivers them from all their troubles.

The Lord is close to the broken-hearted and saves those who are crushed in spirit.

Ephesians 2:13

But now in Christ Jesus, you who once were far away have been brought near by the blood of Christ.

Isaiah 155:6

Seek the Lord while he may be found; call on him while he is near.

Part Three

Philippians 4: 4-9

Do not be anxious about anything

It's an exhortation and also a command. God knows that anxiety is not good for us. If it's a command, then you know God will help you. Anxiety is the perceived loss of control. So, the best way to battle anxiety is to know that it is not us who are meant to be in control. It is God who needs to be in control, and He is!

When governments and world leaders struggle to know what's best to do, we need to hang on to the fact that God is in control. God urges us not to be anxious about anything.

And why doesn't He want us to be anxious? It's because He cares for us and wants the best for us. He knows that being anxious, worrying, and panicking do us no good. He knows how fruitless they are, how they rob us of the peace and joy which He longs for us to have. He doesn't want us to be anxious because He wants us to trust Him.

God knows the end from the beginning. He knows what the future holds for us. We worry about a hundred things that will never happen. God knows exactly what will happen and when. If we can truly trust God, there is no need to be anxious. Just like a child trusting their father when they are worried about something that he knows will be ok, we need to trust God who knows all things.

Remember to…

Trust in God, and see your worries fade.

Actively seek not to worry.

Bible Verses to Meditate on

Matthew 6:25-27

"Therefore I tell you, do not be anxious about your life, what you will eat or what you will drink, nor about your body, what you will put on. Is not life more than food, and the body more than clothing? Look at the birds of the air: they neither sow nor reap nor gather into barns, and yet your heavenly Father feeds them. Are you not of more value than they? And which of you by being anxious can add a single hour to his span of life?"

Matthew 6:34

Therefore do not worry about tomorrow, for tomorrow will worry about itself. Each day has enough trouble of its own.

John 14:27

Peace I leave with you; my peace I give you. I do not give to you as the world gives. Do not let your hearts be troubled and do not be afraid.

1 Peter 5:7

Cast all your anxiety on him because he cares for you.

Part Four

Philippians 4: 4-9

Do not be anxious about anything, but in every situation, by prayer and petition, with thanksgiving, present your requests to God.

...by prayer and petition

Prayer is the most powerful weapon that God has placed at our disposal. Now is the time that we need to use that weapon to its full effect. As someone who has suffered from anxiety and panic for many years, I can tell you that prayer is a wonderful help in bringing oneself to peace. When you use this amazing gift that God has given us - worry, anxiety, and fear can melt away and God's peace will fill our being.

Praying and coming into God's presence have so many benefits for us as humans. Surprisingly, most of them aren't necessarily spiritual, mysterious, or miraculous. I'm not saying these benefits aren't God given, but most pertain to much more mundane things. God can and does meet with us in wonderful and mysterious ways in prayer. He can fill us with a peace that is beyond our human understanding. He can answer us in miraculous ways, and He can speak to us as we listen to Him in prayer. All of these things can help relieve our anxiety. However, there are also other ways that prayer can help our troubled minds.

Prayer helps us to stop. In the busyness of our lives, especially the life of our thoughts, prayer helps us to stop, take a breath, and focus on something more useful. Prayer is relaxing; we can find a safe place that is quiet and comfortable. We can take time to relax into spending time with our Heavenly Father. God is always happy to listen. Offloading our concerns in the presence of God is a very therapeutic thing to do. Asking for God's perspective helps us to see our worries and fears for what they are. I know most of my worries and fears are my over-reacting to something or blowing things out of proportion. When we see these things in the context of an Almighty God who loves and cares for us, they can easily take on a much less significant role in our lives.

Remember to...

Not agonise over your problems - but pray about them. God is much more capable of dealing with your issues than you are.

Take your problems to God on your knees before the weight of your problems drives you to your knees.

Bible Verses to Meditate on

Ephesians 6:18a

And pray in the Spirit on all occasions with all kinds of prayers and requests.

1 John 5:15

And if we know that he hears us—whatever we ask—we know that we have what we asked of him.

Psalm 37:4

Take delight in the Lord, and he will give you the desires of your heart.

Psalm 20:5

May we shout for joy over your victory and lift up our banners in the name of our God.

May the Lord grant all your requests.

Part Five

Philippians 4: 4-9

Do not be anxious about anything, but in every situation, by prayer and petition, with thanksgiving, present your requests to God.

...with thanksgiving.

Whatever our circumstances, whatever difficulties we face, whatever problems are weighing us down, we all have so much for which to be thankful. When we are thankful, we enter God's gates. It is always good to express our thanks to God in prayers similar to the one below. When we pray such prayers we enter into the peaceful presence of God.

Lord,

we thank you for our homes,

places of refuge, comfort, warmth, and security.

We thank you for loved ones to care for us,

look out for us, talk to us and reassure us.

We thank you for the love You have put within us

to care for others; family, friends, and strangers alike.

We thank you for Your provision;

we thank you that we have enough.

We thank you for our leaders

who are working on our behalf to keep us safe,

making the best, though tough, decisions for all concerned.

We thank you for our Health Care Services

and all who work within them;

working tirelessly to treat the ill and the dying.

We could go on, but Lord, finally,

we thank you for Your peace

and the comfort of Your Spirit.

Help us to turn to You

and to fight fear with faith.

Amen.

Life is tough for many, but if we stop and look, we all have things for which we can be thankful. I know it might not always seem that way; life can be really tough! However, no matter how bad things get, at the very least, we have Christ. We have an Eternal friend, a Saviour, Redeemer, Counsellor, Guide, Lord, and Heavenly Father. With Christ, we have more than enough. Christ can never be taken away from us: no earthly circumstance, no economic downturn, no one's mistakes, no angry boss or illness can separate us from Him and all He longs to be for us. The Bible is very clear on this. Romans 8:38-39 states...

For I am convinced that neither death nor life, neither angels nor demons, neither the present nor the future, nor any powers, neither height nor depth, nor anything else in all creation, will be able to separate us from the love of God that is in Christ Jesus our Lord.

Now that on its own is enough for which to be thankful!

When we look to Christ with thanksgiving, it helps put our circumstances into perspective. It lifts our eyes from the problem to the solution. It changes our focus from our ever-changing circumstances to our never-changing Heavenly Father. We enter the gates of heaven with thanksgiving. What better place to be if we are feeling worried, anxious, or fearful?

Remember to…

Be thankful in every situation, no matter how tough things get.

We always have things to be thankful for; we just need to make that conscious choice to stop and remind ourselves.

Bible Verses to Meditate on

1 Chronicles 16:34

Give thanks to the Lord, for he is good; his love endures forever.

Psalm 95:2-3

Let us come before him with thanksgiving and extol him with music and song.

For the Lord is the great God, the great King above all gods.

Psalm 100:4

Enter his gates with thanksgiving and his courts with praise; give thanks to him and praise his name.

Psalm 9: 1

I will give thanks to you, Lord, with all my heart; I will tell of all your wonderful deeds.

Colossians 3:16-17

Let the message of Christ dwell among you richly as you teach and admonish one another with all wisdom through psalms, hymns, and songs from the Spirit, singing to God with gratitude in your hearts. And whatever you do, whether in word or deed, do it all in the name of the Lord Jesus, giving thanks to God the Father through Him.

Colossians 4:2

Devote yourselves to prayer, being watchful, and thankful.

Lamentations 3:22-23

Because of the LORD's great love, we are not consumed, for his compassions never fail. They are new every morning; great is your faithfulness

Part Six

Philippians 4: 4-9

Do not be anxious about anything, but in every situation, by prayer and petition, with thanksgiving, present your requests to God.

...present your requests to God.

Presenting your requests to God means leaving them with Him and trusting Him with them. When we trust Him with our anxieties, worries, and fears, He takes the weight out of them - we've given the issue to a more capable person to deal with it.

When we take our pets to the vet who knows far more about animals than we do, we don't hover around watching their every move; we don't grab the pet back and try to cure it ourselves. We trust the vet to do what they are qualified to do and leave them to get on with the job. The same is true with God. Present your request to God and leave it with Him, trusting Him with it.

Many of us are not very good at letting go. For some reason, we like to hang on to things; even things we know are not good for us. We have a problem or a worry, and we like to hold on to it. We may share our concerns with others, but we also want to keep a tight grip on it ourselves. For some of us, we never seem happier than when we have something about which to worry. We may have big worries and massive anxiety, but we have grown comfortable with them. We've put in place coping mechanisms, and sometimes we don't quite know what we would do without a particular concern. But that is not how God wants our lives to be. He knows that the best thing for us is to live worry-free; free of anxiety, and free from fear. He wants us to give our worries to Him and to leave them there.

That is, as you well know, easier said than done. Yet it is possible, and the more we do it, the easier it becomes. If we can learn to trust God with our anxieties, then we can leave them with Him knowing that He is so much better equipped to deal with them than we are. When we give our concerns to God, He can put them in perspective. When we can see them from God's perspective, they don't seem so big anymore.

Remember to…

Leave your worries with God, turn your back on them, and walk away. Leaving your anxieties with God is like turning on the light. They don't seem as scary in the light as they did in the dark.

Walk away and don't turn back. Trust that God is more than capable of dealing with them.

Bible Verses to Meditate on

Psalm 55:22

Cast your burden on the Lord, and he will sustain you; he will never permit the righteous to be moved.

Romans 8:38

And we know that in all things God works for the good of those who love him, who have been called according to his purpose.

Ecclesiastes 3:6

There is a time to search and a time to give up, a time to keep and a time to throw away.

Jeremiah 29:11

For I know the plans I have for you," declares the LORD, "plans to prosper you and not to harm you, plans to give you hope and a future.

Isaiah 43:18-19

Forget the former things; do not dwell on the past. See, I am doing a new thing! Now it springs up; do you not perceive it? I am making a way in the wilderness and streams in the wasteland.

Proverbs 3:5-6

Trust in the LORD with all your heart and lean not on your own understanding; in all your ways submit to him, and he will make your paths straight.

Part Seven

Philippians 4: 4-9

And the peace of God, which transcends all understanding, will guard your hearts and your minds in Christ Jesus.

And the peace of God, which transcends all understanding...

If we play our part, God will always play His part. So here we see that if we rejoice in the Lord, show gentleness and calm, turn to God with thanksgiving and ask Him specifically for what we want, He will then respond to us with His amazing peace.

I have come to see this peace in two particular ways. Firstly, this is a peace that is beyond our understanding. It is a peace that occurs when there really shouldn't be peace. It is a mysterious peace that could only possibly come from God. It is a peace in times of trouble, a sense of peace in the middle of a world crisis, a peace where there would normally be fear, anxiety, and panic.

Secondly, it is a peace that bypasses the need for understanding. As humans, we love to figure things out, and until we do, we do not have peace. So many of our anxieties are based on us not knowing the answer. We long to know how things will turn out; will I or someone I love fall ill, will I be able to provide for my family, what happens if I can't work, what is our government going to do next, how should I respond to this or that situation, what does the future hold and so on.

The questions are endless and sometimes just go around and around in our heads as we become more worried, anxious, and fearful. We believe that if we can figure out all the answers, then we will be at peace. God's peace is a peace that bypasses a need for all those answers. It is a peace that comes while all those questions remain unanswered. It is a peace that comes and says you may not have the answers, but you know the One who holds the key to every solution. It is more important to know that God is the solution than to continue to worry over questions that humans may not be able to answer. God's peace comes before the questions are answered, and God's peace is so much better than any answer could ever be.

Remember to…

Not worry about the questions or the answers but to look to God, the ultimate solution.

Play our part and trust God to play His part.

Bible Verses to Meditate on

Colossians 3:15

Let the peace of Christ rule in your hearts, since as members of one body you were called to peace. And be thankful

Psalm 29:11

The LORD gives strength to his people; the LORD blesses his people with peace.

Psalm 85:8

I will listen to what God the LORD says; he promises peace to his people, his faithful servants

Isaiah 26:3

You will keep in perfect peace those whose minds are steadfast, because they trust in you.

Isaiah 54:10

Though the mountains be shaken and the hills be removed, yet my unfailing love for you will not be shaken nor my covenant of peace be removed," says the LORD, who has compassion on you.

John 16:33

I have told you these things, so that in me you may have peace. In this world you will have trouble. But take heart! I have overcome the world."

Part Eight

Philippians 4: 4-9

And the peace of God, which transcends all understanding, will guard your hearts and your minds in Christ Jesus.

…will guard your hearts and minds in Christ Jesus.

Jesus will keep His part of the bargain by building a garrison of peace around your heart and mind. Jesus died so that you may have peace. If we turn to Him, if we move our eyes from our worry to our Saviour, He will place an army around us to protect us from that situation and bring us His amazing peace.

I love the imagery of God's peace guarding our hearts and minds. I picture centurions standing watch, ensuring that nothing can come our way that would cause us to worry. It shows that God takes this seriously. He doesn't want us to worry or be anxious. Though we are living in uncertain times; though we don't know what the future holds; though we may have financial difficulties, be sick, or even lose loved ones, God does not want us to worry. His peace will protect our hearts and minds.

We can stand firm because God is protecting us from fear. For most of us, the worst scenarios we play out in our heads will not happen. God wants to protect us from all that unnecessary concern. He doesn't want us to have sleepless nights over things that will never occur. Therefore, He promises to guard our hearts to save us from those fears.

Remember to...

Focus on the fact that God does not want you to worry. So much so that He guards your heart and your mind to prevent you from doing so.

Be thankful that God wants the best for you, even in these trying days.

Bible Verses to Meditate on

Psalm 51:10

Create in me a clean heart, O God, and renew a right spirit within me.

Romans 12:2

Do not be conformed to this world, but be transformed by the renewal of your mind, that by testing you may discern what is the will of God, what is good and acceptable and perfect.

Proverbs 23:26

My son, give me your heart, and let your eyes observe my ways.

Isaiah 41:10

So do not fear, for I am with you; do not be dismayed, for I am your God. I will strengthen you and help you; I will uphold you with my righteous right hand.

Psalm 46:1

God is our refuge and strength, an ever-present help in trouble.

Psalm 57:1

Have mercy on me, my God, have mercy on me, for in you I take refuge. I will take refuge in the shadow of your wings until the disaster has passed.

1 Thessalonians 5:23-24

May God himself, the God of peace, sanctify you through and through. May your whole spirit, soul and body be kept blameless at the coming of our Lord Jesus Christ. The one who calls you is faithful, and he will do it.

Part Nine

Philippians 4: 4-9

Finally, brothers and sisters, whatever is true, whatever is noble, whatever is right, whatever is pure, whatever is lovely, whatever is admirable if anything is excellent or praiseworthy think about such things.

So, we have given our worries, anxieties, and fears to God. We've prayed about them with thanksgiving. We've left them with God and trusted Him with them.

We've received His peace, and He has placed an army around our hearts to protect it. So, now we need to stop those thoughts from coming back.

God tells us here how to do just that. After we've cleared our minds of our worries, we fill our minds with good things. We no longer need to focus on our anxieties; we can now focus on the things in our life that are good and pure, noble, admirable, and praiseworthy. A mind that is full of such things has no room for worry, anxiety, and fear. There is no room in a thankful heart for fear.

Even during the worst times in our lives, there are good things on which we can focus. There are always glimmers of light in our darkest days; all we need to do is look for them. Now that can be incredibly hard to do; it can even be painful. However, if we really look, we will find them. If we can focus on them, if only for a little while, we will find strength, hope, and encouragement. Just as we have seen that there is always something to be thankful for; there are always good things on which we can focus. At the very least, we can focus on the goodness of God.

At the end of this book, there are more Bible verses on which you can meditate. Verses that are good, true, excellent, praiseworthy, encouraging, and hopefully helpful to you. If we focus on verses such as these, and stories of people who are good, caring, compassionate, and loving, we don't give worry, anxiety, or fear a chance to get a foothold in our lives.

Remember to…

Focus on things that are good and helpful to our hearts and minds.

Look to God and His word to find things that are true, noble, right, pure, admirable, excellent, or praiseworthy and focus on these things.

Bible Verses to Meditate on

Romans 12:2

Do not conform to the pattern of this world, but be transformed by the renewing of your mind. Then you will be able to test and approve what God's will is—his good, pleasing and perfect will.

Proverbs 4:25

Let your eyes look straight ahead; fix your gaze directly before you.

Colossians 3:2

Set your minds on things above, not on earthly things.

Hebrews 3:1

Therefore, holy brothers and sisters, who share in the heavenly calling, fix your thoughts on Jesus, whom we acknowledge as our apostle and high priest.

Hebrews 12:1-2

Therefore, since we are surrounded by such a great cloud of witnesses, let us throw off everything that hinders and the sin that so easily entangles. And let us run with perseverance the race marked out for us, fixing our eyes on Jesus, the pioneer and perfecter of faith. For the joy set before him he endured the cross, scorning its shame, and sat down at the right hand of the throne of God.

Part Ten

Philippians 4: 4-9

Whatever you have learned or received or heard from me, or seen in me—put it into practice. And the God of peace will be with you.

These few verses hold a wealth of wisdom and practical advice to help us free ourselves from Worry, Anxiety, and Fear. Here, in this final verse, Paul goes further and I will go further still. Paul says that if we follow his teachings and his example and put it into practice in our own lives, then the God of peace will be with us. I say that if we follow the teachings of the entire Bible and follow the example of many people we find within its pages, then the God of peace will be with us. However, if we can just put into practice, the wisdom and instruction found in these few, small, verses, then God's peace will be with us.

The Bible has so much to teach us about peace. So much that is relevant for us today as individuals, families, communities, countries, and indeed the entire world.

Remember to...

Seek out God's wisdom in the pages of the Bible with the Holy Spirit as our guide.

Put into practice all we have learned.

Bible Verses to Meditate on

Job 23:11

My feet have closely followed his steps; I have kept to his way without turning aside.

John 14:6

Jesus answered, "I am the way and the truth and the life. No one comes to the Father except through me.

Proverbs 3:5-6

Trust in the LORD with all your heart and lean not on your own understanding; in all your ways submit to him, and he will make your paths straight

Psalm 119:105

Your word is a lamp for my feet, a light on my path.

A prayer for us all

Dear Lord Jesus,

Help us put into action Your solution for worry, anxiety, and fear.

Let us turn our focus to You, knowing that You are all we need.

Help us Lord to be thankful in these coming days, no matter how difficult life may become.

Let us help ourselves by putting into practice all we have learned in the pages of Your Word.

Help us to be faithful in praying for our world and others.

And may Your peace reign in our lives, in our families, in our communities, in our countries, and in our world.

                We thank you, Lord, Amen

When we become worried, anxious, or fearful, is it very easy for it to become all-consuming. We can turn in on ourselves and let the cause of our concern become our main focus. However, there is another way. It's not always easy, and it takes patience, practice, and perseverance. We can, if we really try, choose to turn from our worry to worship, to turn from fear to faith and from panic to prayer. Prayer is a great way to put our troubles into perspective. Focusing on God is a brilliant way to calm down and bring ourselves peace. Taking our eyes from our troubles to the troubles of others is a great way not only to help others by praying for them but to help ourselves as well. Prayer is a powerful tool in so many ways. It is a great way for God to change us for our own good and for His purposes and glory. Worship also lifts us from our earthly problems to our heavenly solution. Worship can lift the spirit and help us to step away from our problems, if only for a short while. In the following sections, you will find prayers, proclamations of faith, and modern psalms of worship that will help you as you move from worry to worship, from fear to faith, and from panic to prayer.

Prayers

The following prayers will guide you in praying for yourself and your situation. These prayers are designed to lift us and others into the presence of God. They will help us focus on God and His great provision, remembering who He is and what He can do for us. My prayer is that as you pray them for yourself and for others, God will move with great power, bringing peace, provision, healing, comfort, and release.

Remember Who is in Control

Lord, we thank you that You are sovereign over everything.

Even when it looks like everything is spiraling out of control, we know that You are in control.

Help us to trust You and to look to You for Your peace and reassurance.

Amen.

Lord, You are the Creator and Sustainer of this world.

You know everything that is going on.

Nothing is beyond Your gaze or beyond Your control.

Thank you, that You know the end from the beginning.

Thank you, that You never desert us and are always there when we call.

Help us to turn from fear to faith and look to You for all we need.

Amen

Almighty Father, we thank you that You reign supreme over Your world.

Though kingdoms rise and fall; though disease and hardship come and go; though earthly leaders and

governments change; You are unchanging.

You love us and want the best for us in all circumstances.

Be the Lord of our lives now and forever.

Help us to lean on You, for You are more than capable.

Amen

Prayers of Thanksgiving

Father, in the midst of uncertainty, worry, and fear, we ask that you would constantly remind us that we have so much for which to still be thankful.

Amen

Father, we thank you for all the things that we so often take for granted.

O Lord, we come before you in a spirit of thanksgiving now.

Help us always to have thankful hearts no matter what we are going through.

In Jesus' name, we pray.

Amen

Father, we thank you that you are our refuge and strength.

Thank You that we can lean on you in times of difficulty.

We thank you that you will never let us down, will always be there for us, and will be our source of peace and comfort.

Amen.

Lord, I thank you for your presence with me now.

I thank you that no matter how I feel, whatever I am going through, and whether I feel it or not, you are always with me.

You hold me in your grip and never let go.

Amen

Father, I thank you that you know me.

You know all about me, how I feel, how I tick.

Thank You, that you hold the solution to all my worries and concerns.

You know what I find difficult, how I struggle, and how I sometimes feel I can't cope.

I thank you that you still love me exactly as I am.

I thank you that when I feel overwhelmed, you are there for me.

Help me to turn to you at all times.

Amen

Prayers for God's Peace

Dear Lord, I am anxious.

May Your peace fall upon me right now.

Help me to focus on that which does not cause me anxiety.

Bring people to me who are a calming and peaceful influence.

In Jesus' name, I pray.

Amen

Lord, You tell me that You bring a peace that passes all understanding.

It is that peace I ask for right now.

It is so hard to understand what is going on in my mind right now and where it will all lead.

In the middle of this uncertainty, bring Your peace, I pray.

Amen.

Lord, I cry out to You.

My life is in turmoil.

There seems to be confusion and insecurity around every corner.

I don't know what tomorrow will bring, but I trust that You do.

Fill me with Your peace, which will help me cope with whatever comes my way.

Amen.

Father God, I need Your peace today.

My life is full of uncertainty, fear, panic, and anxiety.

My worries pile up, and I feel they will drown me.

Draw near to me, I pray, and help me to draw near to You.

Let me know Your presence with me and bring me to a true sense of peace in my life.

Amen

Lord, it is Your peace I seek today.

I am bombarded with news that causes me to fear for the future.

I am worried about all sorts of things.

I am concerned for myself, my friends, and my family.

Help me to place them in your most capable hands, trusting that you love them even more than I do.

Protect them, I pray and give them Your peace this day.

Amen.

Amidst the worry, anxiety, fear, and panic, Lord bring me peace.

Let my heart and my mind be free of trouble and stress.

May my focus now, be you and you alone.

Bring me into your presence and shelter me under your all protecting wings.

Amen.

Lord, take this panic from me.

Still my mind.

Help me to breathe.

With every breath I take, bring me your peace.

Remove me from all harm.

Help me to rest with you.

Let me focus on you and you alone.

Hold me close.

Help me to know that this will pass.

Let me know deep down that everything is going to be ok.

Amen.

Prayers For Our Minds

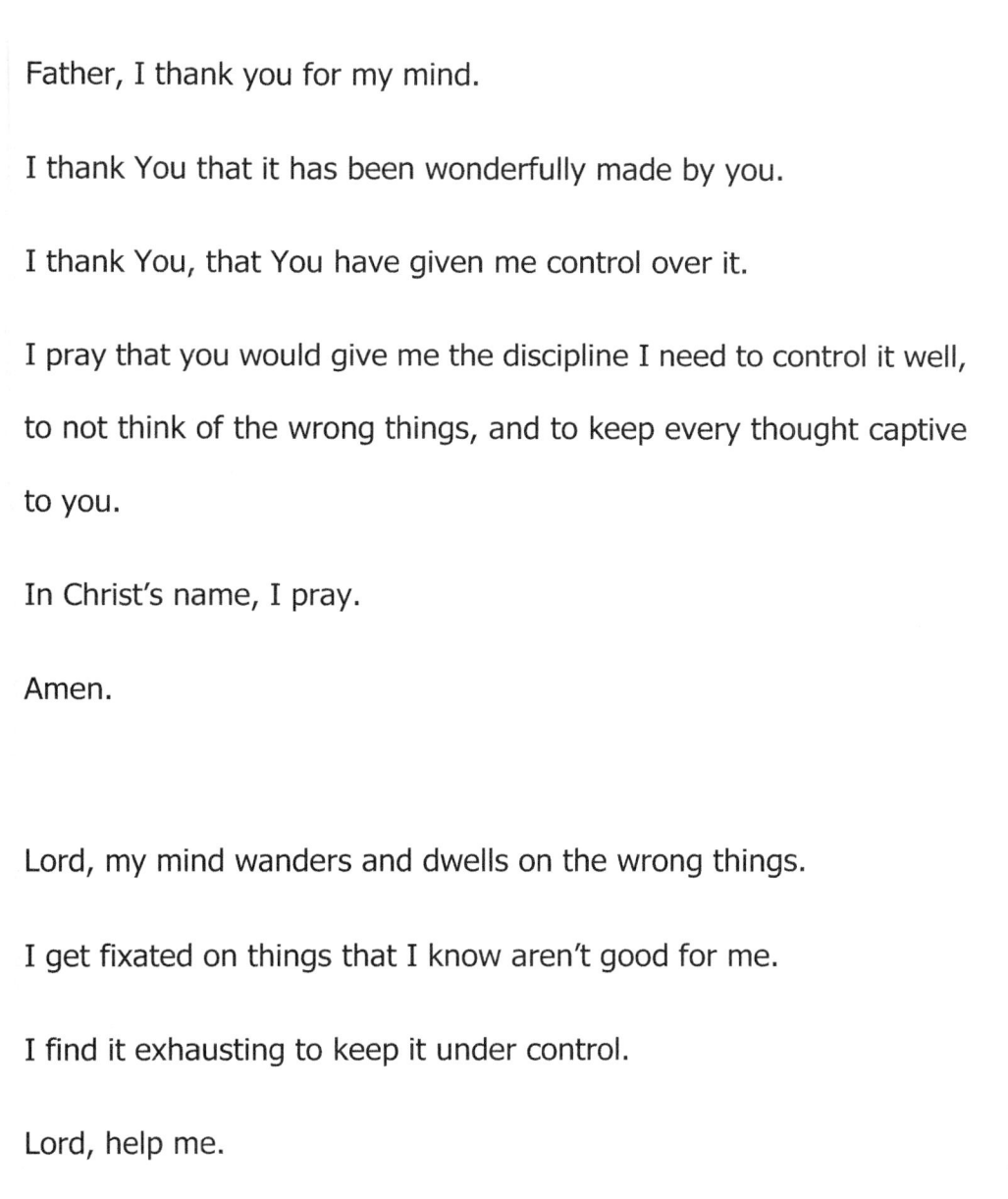

Father, I thank you for my mind.

I thank You that it has been wonderfully made by you.

I thank You, that You have given me control over it.

I pray that you would give me the discipline I need to control it well, to not think of the wrong things, and to keep every thought captive to you.

In Christ's name, I pray.

Amen.

Lord, my mind wanders and dwells on the wrong things.

I get fixated on things that I know aren't good for me.

I find it exhausting to keep it under control.

Lord, help me.

Give me the strength and the focus that I need to keep turning away from that which is wrong and focusing on things that are beneficial for me.

Remind me to continue to do this throughout each day, and at night, bring my mind to rest focused on you.

Amen.

Lord Jesus, my mind is in a dark place right now.

I pray that you would bring your light.

Shine in all the places that need your touch and help me to focus my mind on you.

In Jesus' name, I ask this.

Amen.

Father, help me this day to keep every thought that enters my mind under your control.

Help me to banish unhelpful, destructive, and negative thoughts and instead focus on those

thoughts that are uplifting, positive, and helpful.

Give me the strength and the control to be able to do this.

In Jesus' name, I ask this.

Amen.

Prayers For Distraction

Lord, distract me, I pray.

Break this destructive thought cycle that I find myself in and help me to change my thinking.

Help me to lift my thoughts to you and to change them from destructive to constructive.

In your name, I pray.

Amen.

Lord, I need my mind to be kept active today.

Let there be no room for unhelpful thought patterns.

Keep my mind and my life focused on you and draw me to yourself.

Give me the discipline that I need, to keep refocusing on all that is good and helpful for me at this time.

Amen.

Father, I ask that you would help me to keep every thought captive to you today.

Distract my mind from that which causes it to worry, fear, or panic.

Keep my mind active on good and beneficial things this day.

Be my focus, O Lord, I pray.

Amen.

Prayers for Discipline

Lord, I know that spending time with you and reading your word is good for my anxiety.

Give me the self-discipline that I need to do them more often.

Help me to see the benefits and that these benefits would encourage me to do them more frequently.

Amen.

Father God, it is sometimes exhausting, continually trying to focus on the right things.

Please give me the discipline that I need though, to continue to do this.

Train me in the way that I should think, so that my mind is set on you more than on my fears and anxieties.

Amen.

O Lord, give me the strength and the discipline that I need this day.

You know that I am not finding this easy but that I am trying and so want to succeed in conquering my fears.

Help me Lord, every step of the way.

Help me to know your touch this day.

Amen.

Dear God, I pray that you would help me to be disciplined in the practical things today.

Help me to get the sleep I need so that my mind is more alert to focus on the right things.

Help me to eat well so that my brain has the nourishment that it needs.

Help me to protect my mind from things that will cause it to fear, like the news or unhelpful films.

In all things, keep my mind set on you.

Amen.

Prayers For Help

Father God, I need your help right now.

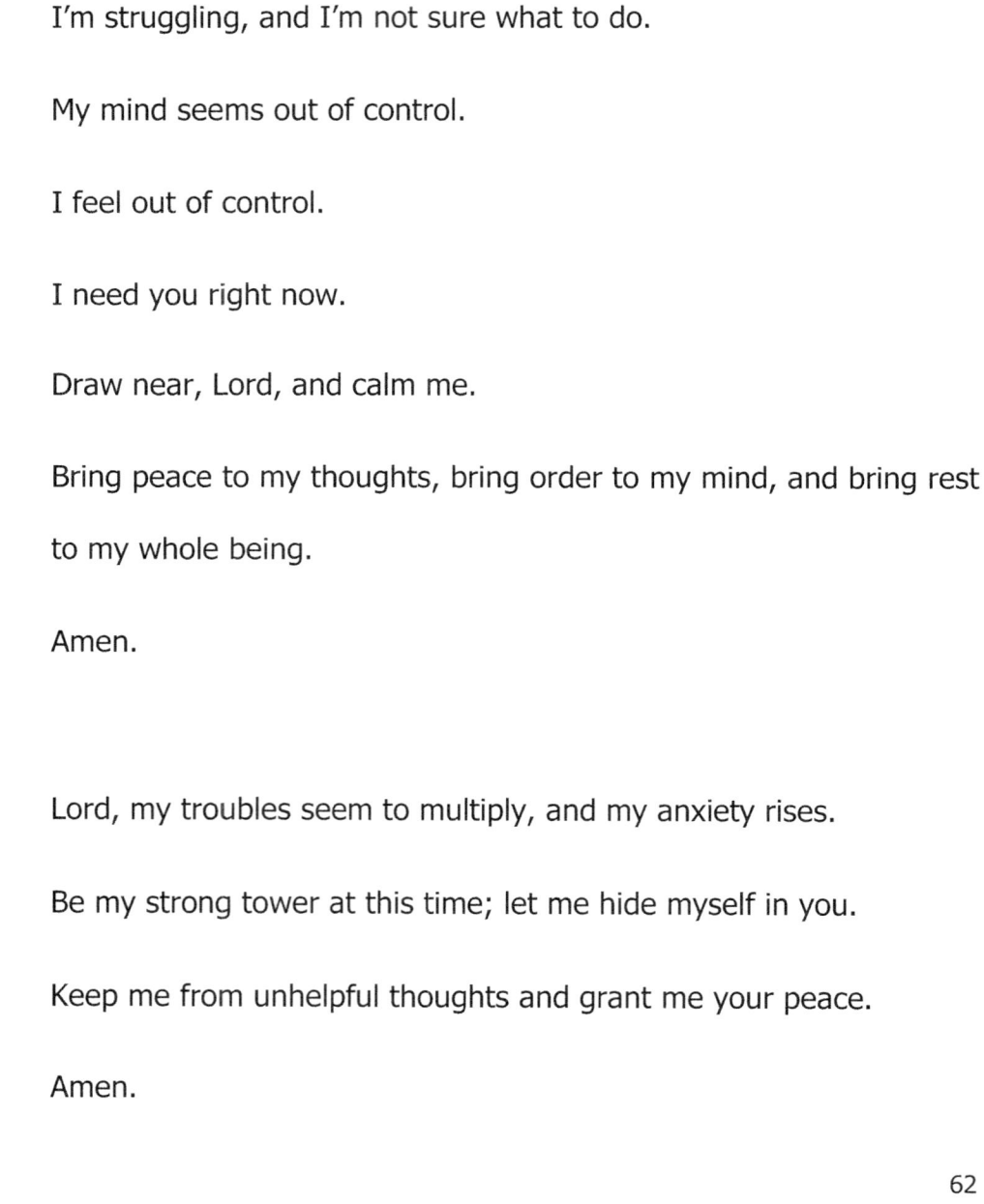

I'm struggling, and I'm not sure what to do.

My mind seems out of control.

I feel out of control.

I need you right now.

Draw near, Lord, and calm me.

Bring peace to my thoughts, bring order to my mind, and bring rest to my whole being.

Amen.

Lord, my troubles seem to multiply, and my anxiety rises.

Be my strong tower at this time; let me hide myself in you.

Keep me from unhelpful thoughts and grant me your peace.

Amen.

Jesus, I come before you now, begging for your help.

You are my only hope.

I need you right now to bring me peace in the turmoil that I now face.

I need your touch of calm in my life.

Everything is frantic, uncertain, and confused.

I can't think straight, and I can't see things changing.

I am lost, and you are my last chance.

Help me, Lord; help me, I pray.

Amen.

Lord, I look to you for help.

Be all that I need of you today, O Lord.

I know I cannot cope on my own.

Draw near to me, Lord, and be my strength and my shield.

Amen.

Prayers For Situations

Father, you know the situation that I face.

You know how it makes me anxious.

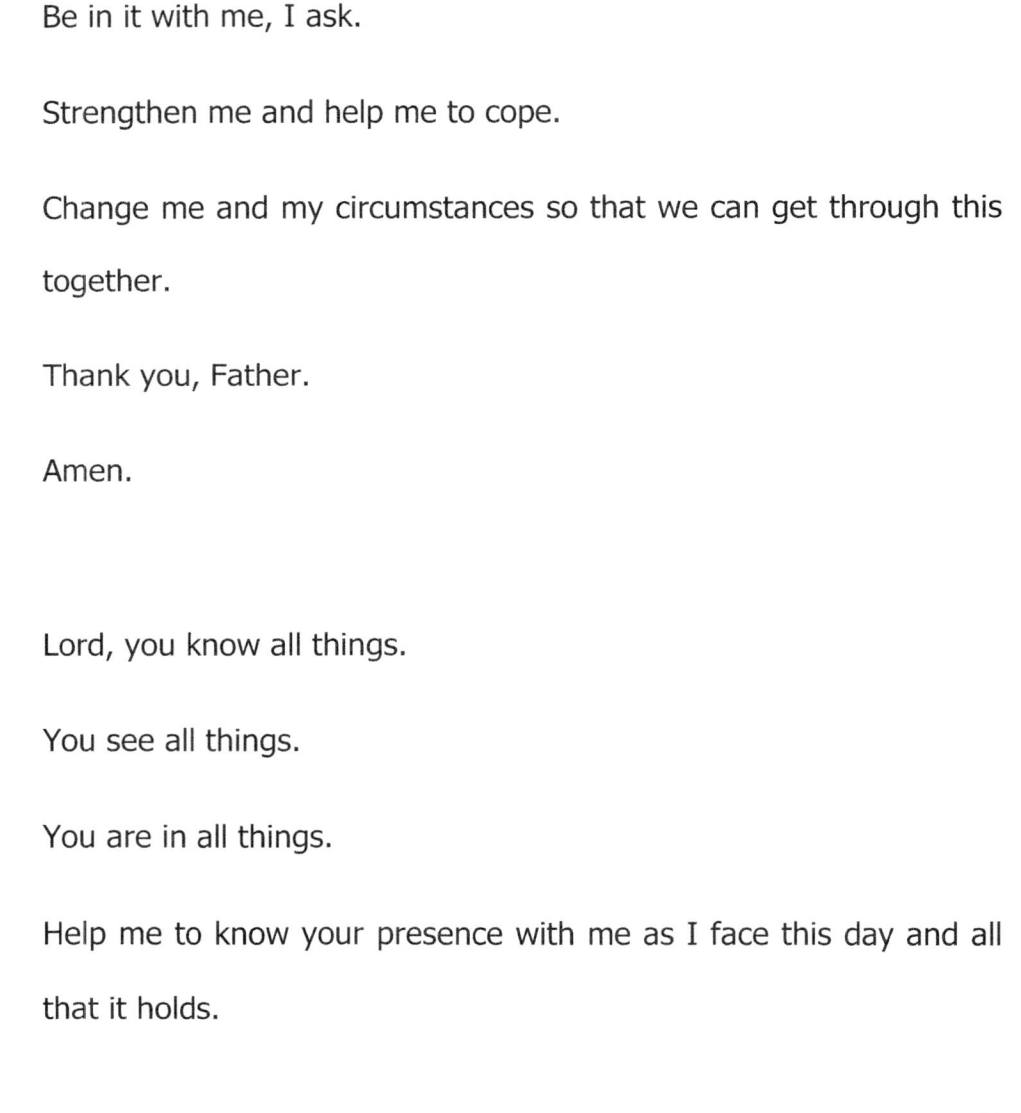

Be in it with me, I ask.

Strengthen me and help me to cope.

Change me and my circumstances so that we can get through this together.

Thank you, Father.

Amen.

Lord, you know all things.

You see all things.

You are in all things.

Help me to know your presence with me as I face this day and all that it holds.

Prepare me for what lies ahead.

Help me not to be anxious about it, but to turn to you and set my focus on your love and care for me.

Be my great Protector and Provider today, Lord, and carry me when needed.

Amen.

Lord, no matter what I face today, I choose to trust you.

Help me to trust you more and more.

Help me to set my focus on you, that you would guide me through this day in peace.

Amen.

Prayers About Uncertainty

Father, we live in uncertain times.

People are facing worry, anxiety, and fear daily.

Not knowing what tomorrow brings is very stressful for many people.

Lord, bring Your peace to troubled minds.

Where there is uncertainty, bring Your everlasting hope.

Where there is fear, bring Your reassurance.

Where there is panic, bring Your comfort.

Help us to look out for each other and face the future step by step, with You by our side.

Amen.

Lord, you know I like everything to be mapped out in front of me.

I want to know how things will turn out, what tomorrow will bring, and what lies ahead in the future.

However, I know life doesn't work like that.

Help me to cope with all the uncertainties of life.

Help me not to be deterred by them but to hold on to You as my support at these times.

Help me to find my security in you and not in my circumstances.

Amen.

Lord, troubles come and go, but You are the same yesterday, today, and forever.

Help me to believe that truth and to hold onto that fact, when the uncertainties of life make me anxious.

Let me not be thrown around by the storm but help me to cling to you, my Rock.

Amen.

Modern Psalms for Worship

Praising God in difficult times helps put our worries into perspective and lifts our thoughts from our troubles to God. There is something peaceful about praising God and recognising all that He has done for us. These modern Psalms are written to help us focus on the right things. I hope you will find that reciting them in times of worry, anxiety, or panic will really help in bringing you to a place of peace.

Praise be to you, O God, all praise is due Your name.

You have given us the gift of life, and we thank You, God, our Father.

We owe You everything; our very lives and so we lift your name on high,

May Your name be praised throughout our world.

Father, I declare that You are my God.

I shout of Your wonderful works.

I just need to look around me to see Your hands at work.

You are so wonderfully creative; everything You turn Your hands to, is amazing.

I give you my praise and my thanksgiving for all that You have given me.

I am Yours, and You are mine.

I love You, and I know that You love me.

I will rest in You now and all the days of my life.

Lord, I hide myself in You.

I thank You that You are all that I need.

Protect me from all harm.

Wrap Your loving arms around me.

I will stay here with You, my Lord, and my God, and I will be thankful.

To You be the glory for all You have made and all You continue to do.

There is nothing that You cannot do.

When I think of You and all You have done for me, I just want to shout out, "Thank You!" but that really doesn't seem enough.

So, I offer You my life as a gift of thanksgiving.

Use me, Lord, in Your great plans.

May my life be a small offering of thanksgiving for all You have done.

Let me say just how great my God is.

Let me tell you everything that He has done for me.

He created all things.

He gave life to every human, animal, and plant on this planet.

He created all this for our delight.

He sustains all things.

He watches over us and continues to love us, even when we really don't deserve that love.

He sent His only son to suffer and die so that we could have eternal life.

How good is that?

How loving is that?

Who else has done anything that even nearly compares to that?

How great is my God?

How great is my God?

My God is love.

Everything He does stems from that.

Everything He does is loving, He can't do anything but love.

He loves me, unconditionally.

Nothing I do can make Him love me more; nothing I do can make Him love me less.

His love is constant.

He could not love me any more than He does right now.

Thank you, Lord, that I am loved.

O God, even in the middle of the darkest night, You are my light.

You shine into the darkness of my situations and reveal your pathway through it.

Come, Lord Jesus, come.

Shine brightly in my life.

Illuminate all parts.

Let there be no darkness found within me.

I will sing of God's goodness, His wonderful grace, mercy, and love.

I will tell of all the amazing things He has done for me, of all He has created for my delight.

I will think about all things that I have to be thankful for; His forgiveness and restoration.

I will shout of all the things He has prepared for me, for the future, for the great hope He sets before me and the place He is making for me in His heavenly Kingdom.

All praise be to God!

All praise be to my God!

I'm excited by what you have in store for me, Lord.

I know you have great plans for me.

Plans for my good and your glory.

I praise You, for you have laid a great future before me.

I can't wait to explore it together with you.

You have taken me by the hand and will lead me onwards.

How brilliant is that, O Lord?

Proclamations of Faith

When life, a situation, or a worry seems overwhelming, it is good to change our focus. If a thought or a train of thought has caused us to worry, panic, or fear, then the best possible solution is to replace those thoughts with different, more positive thoughts. Continuing to focus on the worry or what is causing us to panic is not a good thing. We need to break that thought process and focus on something else. This is easier said than done and takes effort and concentration, but it can be done and done to great effect. There are many ways we can choose to change our thought patterns. One way I found very useful, was to change my mind from focusing on my problems and instead recite a Christian hymn. It was a distraction technique that worked well and not only distracted me but refocused me on God. Another good way is to make a strong proclamation of faith. This is similar to the Christian Hymn but is more of an active choice on what to believe. I find it is turning my back on wrong beliefs and turning towards right and important beliefs. Remember, God doesn't want our lives to be ruled by fear and worry. He doesn't want us to live in a state of panic or anxiety. He has given us the ability to choose what we set our minds on. The following proclamations of faith are great things to focus our minds upon, especially during times of trouble. It might be that you choose one of the following. Memorise it or keep a copy with you. You can then recite it over and over in times of stress, to help bring you to a place of peace.

I believe and trust in You, Father God, Creator, and Sustainer of all things.

I believe You know all things, can do all things, and love all that You have created.

I believe You sent Your only son to earth to die in order to pay the price for our wrongdoings.

I believe and trust in You, Jesus Christ, Saviour of this world.

I believe You were born to show us how to live and died to save us.

I believe You conquered death for us all and rose again.

I believe You returned to heaven so that Your Holy Spirit could come to be our ever-present help.

I believe and trust in You, Holy Spirit, living in us who believe.

I believe You fill us with great gifts, comfort us, convict, and guide us.

I believe You are at work in the lives of all Christians to help build God's Kingdom here on earth as it is in heaven.

I believe God's Kingdom in heaven awaits those who believe.

I believe that this life is not the end; we are only passing through; this is not our home.

I believe that Jesus is preparing a place for us in His heavenly Kingdom, where we will live with Him for eternity.

I trust Lord that, just like the story of Joseph, you can turn my situation around in an instant.

I trust you for what lies ahead.

I trust that you are working your purposes out for my life.

I trust, Father, that you have great plans for me, plans to prosper me and not to harm me.

I trust Lord that you love me and want the best for me in all circumstances.

Help that trust to increase day by day.

I believe that You are at work in my life.

I believe that You have my best interest in mind.

I believe that You love me, unconditionally.

I believe You won't let me down.

I believe You are with me.

I believe You sent Your son to die to save me.

I believe He is preparing a place for me in Your Kingdom.

I believe He will come again in Glory.

I believe I will live with You forever in heaven.

Father, I believe You are here for me.

I believe You want the best for me in all circumstances.

I choose to believe, even when I don't feel your presence, that you are with me.

I believe You will bring me through this, to a place of peace.

I believe You are all I need.

I believe You are my help in times of trouble.

More Bible Verses for Your Peace and Comfort

Biblical meditation is one great way to bring us from a place of worry, anxiety, or fear to a place of peace. The Bible is full of wonderful wisdom and peace-filled verses that can help us in a time like this. Meditating on the Bible isn't complicated and can take on various forms. In its simplest form, it is just about dwelling for longer than you usually would on the words found in a passage. The more time we can take to focus on God's word, the more at peace we are likely to feel. Here is a way that I have found useful over the years...

Read the passage very slowly, almost as slowly as you can. Let the words sink in; every one of them.

Read it again but this time put emphases on different words.

Think about if anything jumped out at you or resonated with you.

What might God be saying to you through these words?

Take those words or a part of the passage that you liked and write them down

Repeat them throughout the day

Pray about them

Below is a selection of Bible verses that I believe may be useful to meditate on, during these difficult days. I'd love to hear your feedback. You can always drop me a line at

<u>nathanhaddockbooks@gmail.com</u>

Numbers 6:24-26

The Lord bless you and keep you;

the Lord make his face shine on you

and be gracious to you;

the Lord turn his face toward you

and give you peace.

John 16:33

I have told you these things,

so that in me you may have peace.

In this world you will have trouble.

But take heart!

I have overcome the world.

Philippians 4:6-7

Do not be anxious about anything,

but in every situation,

by prayer and petition,

with thanksgiving,

present your requests to God.

And the peace of God,

which transcends all understanding,

will guard your heart

and your minds in Christ Jesus.

2 Thessalonians 3:16

Now may the Lord of peace himself

give you peace at all times

and in every way.

The Lord be with all of you.

Psalm 4:8

In peace I will lie down and sleep,

for you alone, Lord,

make me dwell in safety.

Isaiah 26:3

You will keep in perfect peace

those whose minds are steadfast,

because they trust in you.

Hebrews 12:14

Make every effort to live in peace with everyone

and to be holy;

without holiness no one will see the Lord.

Psalm 119:165

Great peace have those who love your law,

and nothing can make them stumble.

Philippians 4:9

Whatever you have learned

or received or heard from me,

or seen in me

—put it into practice.

And the God of peace will be with you.

Romans 8:6

The mind governed by the flesh is death,

but the mind governed by the Spirit is life and peace.

Hebrews 12:11

No discipline seems pleasant at the time,

but painful

Later on, however,

it produces a harvest of righteousness

and peace for those who have been trained by it.

Psalm 29:11

The Lord gives strength to his people;

the Lord blesses his people with peace.

Proverbs 3:1-2

My son, do not forget my teaching,

but keep my commands in your heart,

for they will prolong your life many years

and bring you peace and prosperity.

Hebrews 13:20-21

Now may the God of peace,

who through the blood of the eternal covenant

brought back from the dead our Lord Jesus,

that great Shepherd of the sheep,

equip you with everything good for doing his will,

and may he work in us what is pleasing to him,

through Jesus Christ,

to whom be glory for ever and ever.

Amen.

Psalm 55:16-17

As for me, I call to God,

and the Lord saves me.

Evening, morning and noon

I cry out in distress,

and he hears my voice.

Isaiah 41:10

So do not fear, for I am with you;

do not be dismayed, for I am your God.

I will strengthen you and help you;

I will uphold you with my righteous right hand.

2 Timothy 1:7

For this reason I remind You

to fan into flame the gift of God,

which is in you through the laying on of my hands.

For the Spirit God gave us does not make us timid,

but gives us power,

love and self-discipline.

Psalm 34:17-18

The righteous cry out, and the Lord hears them;

He delivers them from all their troubles.

The Lord is close to the broken-hearted

and saves those who are crushed in spirit.

Colossians 3:15

Let the peace of Christ rule in your hearts,

Since as members of one body

you were called to peace.

And be thankful.

Deuteronomy 31: 8

The Lord himself goes before you

and will be with you;

He will never leave you nor forsake you.

Do not be afraid;

do not be discouraged.

Psalm 23: 4

Even though I walk

through the darkest valley,

I will fear no evil,

for you are with me;

your rod and your staff,

they comfort me.

Psalm 86: 5-8

You, Lord, are forgiving and good,

abounding in love to all who call to you.

Hear my prayer, Lord;

listen to my cry for mercy.

When I am in distress, I call to you,

because you answer me.

Among the gods there is none like you, Lord;

no deeds can compare with Yours.

Psalm 119: 76

May your unfailing love be my comfort,

according to your promise to your servant.

Psalm 9:9

The Lord is a refuge for the oppressed,

a stronghold in times of trouble.

Psalm 46:1

God is our refuge and strength,

an ever-present help in trouble.

Psalm 116: 1-2

I love the Lord, for he heard my voice;

he heard my cry for mercy.

Because he turned his ear to me,

I will call on him as long as I live.

Psalm 119: 48-53

I reach out for your commands, which I love,

that I may meditate on your decrees.

Remember your word to your servant,

for you have given me hope.

My comfort in my suffering is this:

Your promise preserves my life.

The arrogant mock me unmercifully,

but I do not turn from your law.

I remember, Lord, your ancient laws,

and I find comfort in them.

Indignation grips me because of the wicked,

who have forsaken your law.

Lamentations 3: 31-62

For no one is cast off

by the Lord forever.

Though he brings grief, he will show compassion,

so great is his unfailing love.

For he does not willingly bring affliction

or grief to anyone.

To crush underfoot

all prisoners in the land,

to deny people their rights

before the Most High,

to deprive them of justice—

would not the Lord see such things?

Who can speak and have it happen

if the Lord has not decreed it?

Is it not from the mouth of the Most High

that both calamities and good things come?

Why should the living complain

when punished for their sins?

Let us examine our ways and test them,

and let us return to the Lord.

Let us lift up our hearts and our hands

to God in heaven, and say:

We have sinned and rebelled

and you have not forgiven.

You have covered yourself with anger and pursued us;

you have slain without pity.

You have covered yourself with a cloud

so that no prayer can get through.

You have made us scum and refuse

among the nations.

All our enemies have opened their mouths

wide against us.

We have suffered terror and pitfalls,

ruin and destruction.

Streams of tears flow from my eyes

because my people are destroyed.

My eyes will flow unceasingly,

without relief,

until the Lord looks down

from heaven and sees.

What I see brings grief to my soul

because of all the women of my city.

Those who were my enemies without cause

hunted me like a bird.

They tried to end my life in a pit

and threw stones at me;

the waters closed over my head,

and I thought I was about to perish.

I called on your name, Lord,

from the depths of the pit.

You heard my plea: "Do not close your ears

to my cry for relief."

You came near when I called you,

and you said, "Do not fear."

You, Lord, took up my case;

you redeemed my life.

Lord, you have seen the wrong done to me.

Uphold my cause!

You have seen the depth of their vengeance,

all their plots against me.

Lord, you have heard their insults,

all their plots against me—

what my enemies whisper and mutter

against me all day long.

John 14: 26-27

But the Advocate,

the Holy Spirit,

whom the Father will send in my name,

will teach you all things

and will remind you of everything I have said to you.

Peace I leave with you;

my peace I give you.

I do not give to you as the world gives.

Do not let your hearts be troubled

and do not be afraid.

Isaiah 35: 4

Say to those with fearful hearts,

"Be strong, do not fear;

your God will come,

he will come with vengeance;

with divine retribution

he will come to save you."

Isaiah 40:31

but those who hope in the Lord

will renew their strength.

They will soar on wings like eagles;

they will run and not grow weary,

they will walk and not be faint.

Luke 12: 22-34

Then Jesus said to his disciples:

"Therefore I tell you,

do not worry about your life,

what you will eat;

or about your body,

what you will wear.

For life is more than food,

and the body more than clothes.

Consider the ravens:

They do not sow or reap,

they have no storeroom or barn;

yet God feeds them.

And how much more valuable you are than birds!

Who of you by worrying can add a single hour to your life?

Since you cannot do this very little thing

why do you worry about the rest?

Consider how the wild flowers grow.

They do not labour or spin.

Yet I tell you,

not even Solomon in all his splendour

was dressed like one of these.

If that is how God clothes the grass of the field,

which is here today,

and tomorrow is thrown into the fire,

how much more will he clothe you

—you of little faith!

And do not set your heart on what you will eat or drink;

do not worry about it.

For the pagan world runs after all such things,

and your Father knows that you need them.

But seek his kingdom,

and these things will be given to you as well.

Do not be afraid, little flock,

for your Father has been pleased to give you the kingdom.

Sell your possessions and give to the poor.

Provide purses for yourselves that will not wear out,

a treasure in heaven that will never fail,

where no thief comes near

and no moth destroys.

For where your treasure is,

there your heart will be also."

Psalm 94: 19

When anxiety was great within me,

your consolation brought me joy.

Romans 8: 38.39

For I am convinced that neither death nor life,

neither angels nor demons

neither the present nor the future,

nor any powers, neither height nor depth,

nor anything else in all creation,

will be able to separate us

from the love of God

that is in Christ Jesus our Lord.

Proverbs 3: 5-6

Trust in the Lord with all your heart

and lean not on your own understanding;

in all your ways submit to him,

and he will make your paths straight.

Jeramiah 17: 7-8

But blessed is the one who trusts in the Lord,

whose confidence is in him.

They will be like a tree planted by the water

that sends out its roots by the stream.

It does not fear when heat comes;

its leaves are always green.

It has no worries in a year of drought

and never fails to bear fruit.

Matthew 11: 28-30

Come to me

all you who are weary and burdened,

and I will give you rest.

Take my yoke upon you

and learn from me,

for I am gentle and humble in heart,

and you will find rest for your souls.

For my yoke is easy

and my burden is light.

Psalm 55: 22

Cast your cares on the Lord

and he will sustain you;

he will never let

the righteous be shaken.

1Peter 5: 6-7

Humble yourselves, therefore,

under God's mighty hand,

that he may lift you up in due time.

Cast all your anxiety on him

because he cares for you.

Psalm 73:26

My flesh and my heart may fail,

but God is the strength of my heart

and my portion forever.

John 14: 1

Do not let your hearts be troubled.

You believe in God; believe also in me.

Isaiah 53: 4-6

Surely he took up our pain

and bore our suffering,

yet we considered him punished by God,

stricken by him, and afflicted.

But he was pierced for our transgressions,

he was crushed for our iniquities;

the punishment that brought us peace was on him,

and by his wounds we are healed.

We all, like sheep, have gone astray,

each of us has turned to our own way;

and the Lord has laid on him

the iniquity of us all.

Joshua 1: 9

Have I not commanded you?

Be strong and courageous.

Do not be afraid; do not be discouraged,

for the Lord your God will be with you wherever you go.

Romans 8: 28

And we know that in all things

God works for the good of those who love him,

who have been called according to his purpose.

Matthew 5: 4

Blessed are those who mourn,

for they will be comforted.

I really hope and pray that you have found this little book helpful.

I would love for you to review this book on Amazon because your opinion helps others decide whether this is an excellent book for them. Please review at

Printed in Great Britain
by Amazon